W9-AAV-051

W9-AAV-051

BEYOND THE CHAINLINK, A CITY

                    IS THE UNION BETWEEN TWO LOVERS,

AHSAHTA PRESS
BOISE, IDAHO

THE NEW SERIES
#59

NEVER TAKING PLACE

BEYOND

THE CHAINLINK

Rusty Morrison

AHSAHTA PRESS
Boise State University, Boise, Idaho 83725-1525
ahsahtapress.org
Cover design by Quemadura / Book design by Janet Holmes
Printed in Canada

Copyright © 2014 by Rusty Morrison

LIBRARY OF CONGRESS CATALOGING-IN-PUBLICATION DATA

Morrison, Rusty.
[Poems. Selections]
Beyond the chainlink / Rusty Morrison.
pages cm. -- (The new series ; #59)
Some selected poems previously published in various periodicals and journals.
ISBN-13: 978-1-934103-46-3 (pbk. : alk. paper)
ISBN-10: 1-934103-46-2 (pbk. : alk. paper)
I. Title.
PS3613.O7777A6 2014
811'.6--DC23
2013034839

Contents

ONE

TWO

THREE

"History does not refer merely, or even principally,
to the past."

JAMES BALDWIN

"We die because we cannot connect the end
to the beginning."

ALCMAEON OF CROTON, FIFTH CENTURY BCE

ONE

"in the first place death

is our only continuity

division

forever unified

in the second place life

is our particular discontinuity"

INGER CHRISTENSEN, *translated by Susanna Nied*

History of sleep

(A MYTH OF CONSEQUENCES)

The ivy across our back fence tangles gray
into a green evening light.

How a second emptiness
un-punctuates the first.

Disloyal,
we attempt to construct.

An ache will tighten
but not form.

Making impossible
even this upsurge of crows across our sightline.

The Mayans invented zero so as not to ignore even the gods
who *wouldn't* carry their burdens.

Too slippery as prayer, too effortless
as longing.

Our problem was preparation. Premeditation
neutered any rage potential.

Years later, the spine of our backyard
appears to have always been crooked.

White jasmine, dove-calm in the lattice, is not
a finely crafted lure.

Impulse says

a little hurt is worth the long, thin fracturing you can use as horizon.

An ignored preoccupation will lick its fur
in the opposite direction.

Rain overflooding a sewer's grate—
stumped, gasping.

Every color your white wall receives
from the concealed world.

Warning: The migration turns
just as it threatens to become visible.

Strategy: What you can't pass through—
let it pass through you.

As opposed to "make do," which is only interested in repeating itself.

Necessities

Fermented liquor of your listening; emptied cup of my vowels.

Kept my old comb, its teeth bent to the shape of both our scalps.

The science is always growing better right beneath what the mind builds to cultivate it.

Interrogators into the constitution of our stone deposits add their own indentations.

All sailors in our intricate sentence, no captain.

Showcased for you, in a shoebox.

The journalist's temptation of measuring meaning against the display ads.

Winter months, the cigarette unlit, ambivalent, but without the least hedge of confusion.

Start from any, even the vilest word.

A study of what strands us.

Inventions

Sanctity in jay's bark; no sanctuary.

They, the dangerous ideas, are following me—their subtle, then unsubtle pointing.
As they keep themselves un-inventoried, disinterested in my scrutiny.

Ears ringing as I look down; dangerous height I've tossed my body this time.
Still, you climb. Let suspicion watch.
A little wind this morning, whittled down from wanton.

Climbing means leaning with and against the guide wires, rhythm of our simplest sense.
Watch-wren chirruping loud.
Which describes the world.
Primed a good from the otherwise spiteful irrelevant; sun in its cloud hat.

Sensework

Because dusk begins

as dirt under my fingernails,

I court the dirt. A body.

I learn it

by watching earth court sky,

absorbing each chord of rain into a chorus of groundwater.

I hum it, low in my throat.

In my ears, small bells—

my body is wet with the chiming arrival of evening fog.

Backward rowing

"ARE THERE BONES HERE?"

——JAKE BERRY

A reappraisal of the hero versions.

My flame-keeping. Talk from the interior crowd
around the not me.

There's an airplane drone about it, a wanted poster.
Maybe a war wound.

The unnatural of any two likenesses,
corresponding in cursive.

Postage due.

Be responsible, I say to myself, optimistic but alert.

Now congenial, now implacable.

All clicks in the lock, keeping me outside the silent-eyed
simpler witchcraft of making day.

Gaiety sometimes along the chalk-lined hopscotch.

Token in my pocket. I know the exact tremble
to lean toward, not to test.

Practiced. All the teenage of my capabilities.

And still blind obedience to the calling-in for supper.

Its just-in-the-nick and spill of
rush-want.

Always a calling, sung along the myriad mother variations.

Which are replicable anywhere. As if they make up
the only world.

And supper replies with the oldest lessons.

Orderly power consumption.

                        Little bites. A short-pronged fork, a blunted knife
                                    to carve and carve.

But never very far into the denser nobody.

                        Which is still my own, my only.

History of expression
(THE TRIED, THE TIRED)

I say "your eyes."
But first light has fallen from them.

I say "our bodies."
But no outline holds.

This schoolyard.
Children run. Too fast to catch.

They bounce the bright round housefire-shipwreck-
lightning-strike

just once
upon the chill ground.

I miss it.
And they laugh.

Beyond the chainlink, a city
is the union between two lovers, never taking place.

A theory of the idyllic is built upon
its refusal to embrace us.

Desire says

here is body—magnolia blossoms, blue veined with a noise

like ants in a line. All the hungers of being
move.

So easy, to people this proposition. People,
the obvious transgression.

How meanings settle upon the eye. Moths in butter.
Contradiction is devotional.

Warning: Have no
easy gods.

Any fact of body is a Braille. Not of touch
but smoother.

Like saying "once,"
and meaning it.

Strategy: Let magnolia petals fall from your

many mouths. Let a moth's fluttering

melt on your tongue. The body
is a delicate continuum, constructed

of anniversaries remembered only in stairwells
and the phrases

you can't forget
in a book you will never find again.

Sensework

I lean

on my body, hard enough to feel its resins crack.

I court the cracks.

Squeeze every breach.

What leaks is, at its end, stifling and sweet. Patience, patience. The dead-animal

smell will be the last trailing hem

of outbreath. The body is a cosmos

of hidden atmospheres—each with its own ravage

to erupt. Every loss

is my accomplice.

Necessities

In through our bedroom window, the full dawn-scape concusses.
Difficult to sustain sleep's equilibrium of wordlessness.
Naming anything, like stepping barefoot in wet sand up to my ankles.
Name after name, sinking me farther beneath waking's buoyancy.

House, this morning, is pale with the rush of what night siphoned off.
Objects, still emptied of resemblance, hum their chord-less cantos.
Bloodless, my knuckles knock on walls without echo, testing singularities.

Sun on the cutlery offers an ageless sheen.
Though it ages the silver relentlessly.

New, but still rudimentary tools to be gleaned from my over-used weaponry.

Inventions

I hear a story-noise start up in my throat.

Teach me the future intricate
I'll teach you the path primitive.

We clear away the dinner dishes, just one cup left for each of us.
I curl into mine, a small cave.
How to animate the amniotic between us?

A softer commotion now, water fretting over the stones of a brook we thought long dry.
I bundle all my slender resurrections, presenting them to you as a bouquet.
Amid tariff and back-debt, you collect, like a deranged actuary.
Offering ecstatic calculus.

Backward rowing

"SO THE OUTSIDE SPEAKS
BY THE DUMB GRACE OF AN OLD WOUND"
—JAKE BERRY

We were talking about the unfinishable,
not the unfinished.

That giving us a vantage point, as we saw it.

But not the advantage.

Beside us sat the pure, indestructible
nostalgia, which remembers nothing and calls it beautiful.

And beside that—dense and hedged, as if drawn in with
crayons—stood my realization about limits

that I nearly, but never
return to.

Listening has everything to do with location.

                                    Comprehension is as circular as sky
            coming around to white, which is not the color of this painted ceiling.

There is a "white as bones"
and then there is a "white as bones bleached prophetic."

                              We have to count them all, count them differently,
                                  line them up right here, like a good list.

We must formulate precisely.

                              And formulations crack the glass under my feet.

But only to flatter the fear in me.

Sensework

The body is a sky falling.

Quick, like a safety-pin snapped open,

little death gaps appear in the cloud-cover,

atmospheric with old narratives: "Once upon a time,"

I tempt with, "Once upon a body lost,"

as if telling could entice what's lost

to listen.

Guile says

                                                               displace the subject

                                                     with objects.
As if to substitute "displace" with "display."

                                                Strategy: Bring roses.
                                             Blossoms expound

                      thorn, plush, perfume, blush—two dozen
                                   long-stemmed rhetorics

                                  exuding perceptual excess,
while securing positional obfuscation.

                                         No more flagrant
                                        than flowery words

                          that blithely neglect their sentence.

History is hidden in fact

(UNTIL AN UPSURGE FROM THE CURRENT)

There was milk in our cruelty.
This was wasteful.

This mistake might find a breeze stirring dry leaves
on the sidewalk.

Here is the egg to fertilize,
not dominate by gesture.

This mistake will not be made
the same way twice.

In a dialogic creation of meaning, everything
must be eaten up.

Send light back through looking for what else color might
become.

A whiskey bottle, bread crumbs, full moon, all of our icons,
like traffic, hellbent on getting somewhere.

A thing caught in the midst of whatever I try to name.

In whatever kind of story you wanted to hear.

I wanted to knock on the door
and make a creek fill with trout.

What changed was my method of breathing, not
the atmosphere.

This mistake
I repeat countless times.

Backward rowing

"COVERING RANDOM DEATH WITH RANDOM LIFE."

—INGER CHRISTENSEN, *translated by Susanna Nied*

To examine a dead thing.

                    The unreality of this touching burns.

The gull's breast is cold.

          One wing lies fully extended. The beak, closed. The eye
                    a still, liquid anonymity.

Despite my kitchen precision.

         I follow the expenditures of gray, limitless
                  in each strewn feather.

I travel the small pain behind my ear. Concede to an invasive,
perhaps usable, dismay.

        Can I taste the canny willfulness of presence?

What it repeatedly fails to expose?

                                    Have I already entered the blind room,
                                        a room of nodding and obeisance?

Cheeks hollow, devotional. My forehead, painted red?

                            The small pain behind my ear contradicts thought.
                                                An elite usability now.

It is the proper distance from which to appreciate
the dead thing.

                                                    How it moves.

Sensework

I court the way a stadium

empties.

The way a stalled freeway stutters forward

its engine-burn and exhaust.

I court the slow hour, the resist and snarl

underneath each busy thought.

I court its sediment's

dismemberment.

The thick crayon that will corrupt intended outline.

Court the way a child can get into a car

and trust any kindly offered going, even one that's standing still.

26

TWO

"The field becomes oblivion when I speak it"

JAKE BERRY

Begin again

Storied out of ourselves.
To start
is a home

crossed out
in neat Xs
making the field

fail wherever the lines stop.
Wherever the lines stop,
color in sky.

I will draw in the moon
from your eyes.
One pupil full,

one void of its course.
Dividing the difference down to zero
is sight.

To draw on what won't be seized
is presence.
All beginning as hoax.

But saying so
grows risky and quickly
elsewhere.

Were you expecting the mirror story again?
Our poor collaboration with language,
otherwise known as eternity.

History of seed

(AN INVERSE OF SHINING)

Our thirst is sunless in a garden
bending backwards.

Unbutton one at a time, you tell me,
use both hands.

Summer is lazy with rumor,
admits nothing.

A little sweat
won't satisfy the girl in my refusal.

Girl with a stick. She tore the petals, not I,
tearing the petals. One by one.

My other, you tell me. The given that we are
bending backwards.

Not the task of illusion.
Just tamp down this soft, freshly moistened soil.

Illusion is chained to law,
not agriculture.

Watching, we won't see leaves break through the smooth
finality of surface.

Still, we sense limit
budding with bewilderments.

No exact moment. But in the wideness
across time, a kind of sieve.

Impatience says

in your hurry, you will only parse the possible

along your private calendar's
predetermined lines.

A saucer of milk left on the back porch
only to hasten night.

Every "if only"
is soaked in the same color.

Strategy: Here is this moment,
its fulcrum is changelessness,

even as sky darkens
and the net of time scoops you up,

like a fish,
into another element.

A wheel of birds
you'll never see

turning south
along a narrow edge of morning light.

Scratch the itch in "fix,"
down to its mineralized emptiness.

Daylight, mistaken for Turnpike.

Sensework

An eye's pupil is black

with all the object-life that lives in the eye

undiscovered.

Black with the impossibility of reflecting back

to every object

its share of eternity

arrested.

In the mirror, the gravel is deceptively thick

on the inward-travelling path—

step in, and it's quicksand.

Necessities

A robin, once, outside our kitchen window, never twice.
You suggest we sever our top floor from normal operations
and go there to visit our premonitions of flight.
In our closets, I throw my shadow ahead of me, like a searchlight.

If you collect my words, don't lose the outline that gave my thought a shape.
If I test for soft spots in your syntax, it's to feel for your pulse.
A medicinal listening can't be bartered or bought.

This isn't my face, just a displacement of space that my thinking makes.
My parody starts whenever I turn to watch myself.

We are stingy with our store-bought, waste what our cloud-watch taught us.

Inventions

Who will captain, once I expose my mutinous lower deck?

This wanting, a pocket mirror I'll rub
until the silver backing rubs off.

Sighting hawks hidden in wan couplets.
Burying my ragdolls in evening's last
quicklime light.

The less divided my gesture,
the more kaleidoscopic the impact of its touch.
Not inviting silence as shield or pawn—simply bare,
when I bare it, open-armed.

Backward rowing

"A DIRECTION (THICK WITH FROST)"

—INGER CHRISTENSEN, *translated by Susanna Nied*

Anaximander tells us things pay to each other a penalty
for the injustice of becoming.

                            Photo of a horse's eye that I carry into my dream
                                      isn't the eye I carry out again.

What do we have that hasn't already met
its giving back?

                            Ridiculed by the least ownership.

The missed realm
chained to my ankles.

                            A tiny calendar, taped to my tongue.

Apples in a bowl have fluency
without need of sequence.

To compete, you tell me, derives from the Latin

competere meaning "to seek together."

Two yellow chairs turn the walls a blue
that couldn't exist without them.

Sensework

I install wisps of straw in the damp beach-sand

to court wind. Impermanence—

too long a word for what spins

inside its syllables, what sparks.

The air today has no blade in its right hand, its left

hidden behind its back.

I court the avalanche

first glimpsed in any quick down-drift of afternoon fog.

History of exposition
(SURFACES SUCCUMB)

In your eyes, I see our city of
polished chrome and mirrored windows

borrowing sky,
multiplying the departures routes

either of us might take.
That's one way to tell it.

Good stories
know how to leave the point behind

many times.
My lips are one example.

Your smile
is hurting me now.

Another building explodes.
Destruction

is not beautiful.
It is the price of expansion.

Vulnerability says

the silhouette of pines against midnight skyline

is spiked,
like any longing to escape.

Warning: World's edge shifts
as if with its own sentience.

Roll your tongue inside your mouth.
Sensations, not the edges, meet.

As if the worst thing you've done
is already forgiven—

the cool of this windowpane,
the blue of this china cup.

Strategy: Not giving it shape, but giving in to the shapes
you've become.

What should be kept, besides compassion for the vanity
of idea?

Only the "coming to" in seeing—

Backward rowing

"IT WAS TO BE LIKE BEING
IT WAS WHAT IT WAS"
—INGER CHRISTENSEN, *translated by Susanna Nied*

Where to look?

                                        Not inside, but right next door
                                            to the awareness factory

that keeps running well-oiled and quiet.

                                        Fastened sometimes to want.

Unbutton river, get canary,
lose violin. Then termites emerge from the light switch.

                                                What liberation
                                                    isn't.

The politics of buying my marriages small—

                            to make-up, to chocolate, to the nameless incessant
                                            I never quite live up to.

Or finish.

                              Silhouette behind the emergency or window glass
                                                    before the calm.

Literal as the cat asleep on the bed

                                                              in the home
                                        I've buried in retellings.

Sensework

Not the lilting, crane-fly silence of memory

but silence compressed into the finality

of iron—

element left when a dying star has consumed its fuel.

Necessities

You tear your toast in pieces, busily amassing crumbs.

I stand at a sink I've emptied of dishes, waiting for the least acknowledgement.

Kitchen formica, flat-lining our inflections.

Luxurious, the look-away.

Threadbare, the turn-back.

I am damp with unused sweetness.

I could run a comb through your glib familiarity.

Its slicked-back shine is mockery.

Out the window, cloud colors shift between telepathy and delusion.

Crow on the phone pole, haughty with inexplicable diction.

Inventions

I hear the vigor and turn, in time, to see moonrise.

Recognition cinders so quickly to semblance.
Blackens into a blind-spot.

Lie down in the grass, let dusk's moisture soak inside my machinations.
The flit of a sparrow, a flint-struck spark my eyes involuntarily shy from.
How long to let perception fledge?

A fluid attention lets instinct turn, quick as a lizard's eye.
Heard the ardor with which pebbles perfect their shape under my feet.
Sudden, between shrubs, set high and plumped:
a fox's tail, a first language.

Backward rowing

"CAUGHT IN A PROVISIONAL GAME. REDUCED TO RESTRAINED DETAILS
THAT CEASELESSLY SINGLE THEMSELVES OUT."
——INGER CHRISTENSEN, *translated by Susanna Nied*

We tidy up the history for visitors.

The aggressive catastrophe will hurry-up, but won't finish.

This intensifies our need to explain. But have we grown more precise
or merely more instructive?

First, we ate our mice at the table, now we scramble after them on the floor.

Crib-death of the gesture.

The debate as to whether or not our degradations are
voluntary does change the bedding.

But leaves our stains intact.

Rattlesnakes, I heard you say.
One dozen, large.

Our agreements have become suspect, but not susceptible.

                                        If poisonous, they must be stonefish.

The hurly-burly of our outcries will only sound against
the medium's steely inertia.

                        On the other hand, nearly every system in our bodies
                                        is affected by weightlessness.

Tonight, the parade.

Sensework

Egret. Heron. White bird. *Egretta garzetta* in the Old World.

Any words for it, an empty nest.

Desultory within its own anonymous inventories,

inventing the day

that surrounds it.

I have no habitat.

How to be, again, a birthed form, sinuous with existence?

THREE

"the cells are words

  a language

  that tells

  that the body

  can waken

  the dead

  how

  a language

  that tells

  that caresses

  can waken the dead

  how

  a language

  that tells the abyss

  between us

  is filled

  how"

INGER CHRISTENSEN, *translated by Susanna Nied*

Begin again

How brittle, our little
endless wait
to achieve in each other
a perfect vanishing.

Under the guise of nerve,
fear blinds us
to the mirror in an offered word.
Begin again.

This time,
we'll make no one
the darling.
No one the terror.

Scrubbed nearly colorless, our dead exhale
a long, approving sigh.
The way beauty
wouldn't.

This time, I'll rub my breath hard
against hope,

until its emptiness
ignites.

Rub your breath hard
against mine—
let any spark be antiphon, arriving as
neither angel nor annihilation.

History of quiet
(BUT NOT WITHOUT RETORT)

Failure is any saying.
Devastated patience along the edge-shine of moonrise.

My silence is all of its own,
but outward turning.

Then the prickly-numb you call endurance.
Possum-eyed empty sleep we'll soon lose night to.

But we are long in our surely genuine,
which we slowly unfurl.

Wild lily of inexactitude.
A blush traffics just above each petal's

arch and curl.
Not idea,

with its way of speaking
farther and farther from itself.

But here is our accident of reasons,
all the names we've given hands to.

What will save us from the intricate contestations
we call discernible world?

This kiss,
outside whatever meaning

I've held
too long,

beyond even wanting.
These lips,

which are not lilies.
Open your eyes,

and I'll open mine—
sky is wearing for us

her long dress of sunset.

For anyone.

Sensework

A brewer's sparrow lands on a low branch.

His notched tail flicks down. All the atmosphere of earth

responds—pure forces of reception

are the black streak on a white pigeon's wing that you didn't

see, don't forget, sleeker gloss of meaning

than thought.

Like the sparrow's multi-ligatured trilling

linking its vowels with ghosts.

Patience says

feel your tongue's silence deep in its root.

Inchoate
isn't necessarily imprecise.

Getting undressed won't
expose the dispute's solution,

but could rouge
a few of its referents.

Warning: Blindering the horse won't make it easier
to pull forth the luminous idea-wagon.

Strategy: Bring down the scaffolding,
put away the paint cans, clean off the brushes.

Then, color expands.

Backward rowing

"FORCES IT ALL TO HAPPEN. IT HAPPENS."
—INGER CHRISTENSEN, *translated by Susanna Nied*

Into our fastidious rock garden, we tweeze event.

> Lock the screen door to watch our neighbors argue
> on their front porch steps.

Keychain-troll to ward off tragedy.

> How to assess our anxiety over VISA payments
> and too much late night TV?

My new sundress is neither the solution nor the absurdity,

> but in the afterlife, I want to remember your hands
> helping me unbutton its buttons.

This *is* eternity, whisper the extras—
tonight, in black and white; tomorrow, Technicolor,

as they sink the Bismarck, stream under the Arc de Triomphe,

jeer the gladiators.

How to make amends for our meager grasp
of mortality?

No help from explanation, which always behaves badly.

Squirming in its fictive seat.

Necessities

Along my sightline, you've set up your carnival.
Your offered smile.
Or are you selling me back my own,
as souvenir?

Always a direction to the thrust of our cryptic silences.
A moss, discernible by mental touch,
predicts which way is true north.

Words fill our lungs with the dust
we eventually will become.

Each exhale must choose anew to release its hostages.

Inventions

At sunset, clouds thick as poultices.

My afternoon of foraging the phenomenal
has rendered the hidden medicinals only more invisible.

I taste the condensation of pine in night-wind: a migration
along bridge-less byways. How to travel
like stars in their milk robes,

like scent, clandestine, and everywhere apparent?
Tomorrow, I will walk more gingerly
among the all-sensing earthworms and all-seeing mud.
Sun on my face, a climate to lift crocuses.

Sensework

How to amass the body's losses,

link its deities together?

In the hot-wiring of bees around a flower's scent,

in the sting on the tongue of sweat.

Backward rowing

"FIGURES IN METAL
VOIDS IN THE CLAY"
—JAKE BERRY

I ask for omens, but I won't be grateful for them.

Gloves too thick to wear. Milk spilled on the mirror.

One long thick white hair just where, as a child, I imagined
I'd grow one.

As if it were an achievement, we explain ourselves.

Without the least curiosity left in it.

There was a certain tree we'd gone looking for,
then it started to rain.

The problem was not the kind of tree.

But why one umbrella could never be large enough.

And two would feel like all the longing in childhood

that reason makes only more inexplicable.

What brings us back?

Strangely sensate resistance of the word "you"
to what we mean by it.

Necessities

Sky, this morning, is donning its white smock.
An awareness that I can see we share,
though we each
wear it differently.

Nothing required of me,
which is a hand-knit never-finished
astonishment.

Stillness extends its meaning to encompass
even the oak branches' moving leaves.

Saturated with calm, my silence unspools its silk.

Inventions

Astringent wind, my adequate face wiped raw.

Weed-heads lean and sway beside the streambed.
Pungent, seed-heavy as sacrament.

In the air, a sentience, scent of spores.
I perform mindlessness before the marsh's wild grasses
as if to gain their confidence.

A heron's sudden rise directly into winter sun
that my eyes can't follow
fills my throat with a vibration
I can't sound out, or swallow.

Backward rowing

"DARKNESS HAS ITS HARMONIES
BRILLIANT AND UNFIXED"
—JAKE BERRY

I name the dog howling
and prevent his conversion to stillness.

While meaning fills its fact, let's play a little lottery
with what's missed.

Words are such a thickness.

Stranding us between too much and too much.

I want to hear our body
of silence, not my speaking voice,

not read from the book we've already built,

which obscures the inner story—
its continuous firmament

                                                         displacement.

As a listener, I won't retain

by absorbing, but by being absorbed.

                                                              Being

sucked through.

Sensework

A gull's shadow on sand.

That's where I'll dig, wanting underwork, not aura.

Not the stiff pelt of what vision captures.

My palms deep in warm sand,

their action pearled, sealed in privacy.

Grace says

and the sound of its saying will gather unto itself
every resonance from everywhere

you hadn't understood
was speaking to you.

To ask
is water

absorbed
into water.

"You," as if it had always been
"I."

Warning: This shine will never be groomed
from glitter.

The void, which forgets itself,
becomes speech.

Emblem,
if tied too tightly to itself.

While grief
continues to people its every expanse.

This reciprocity
won't concentrate.

"I," as if it had always been "you."

History of structure
(INCONSPICUOUS AND CONTINUOUS, ITS UNDULATIONS)

Edge is a wisdom word, as far as it goes.
Yet I fail to step back. Even momentarily.

Folding chairs crouch in their stack.
Traffic lights offer in sequence

their small, stunned vanishings.
There is a bronze placard that declares

all history a matter of interpretation.
I wanted to take a yellow cab

without actually having to speak.
When you look out the window

you can't help but escape from the subject.
Except in the case of painting.

As mysteriously as they came,
you answer.

What is being preserved here? I ask.
What is being preserved

is here,
you answer.

I move our reasons
back inside the classroom.

Which isn't about our sorrow
for what remains uncontainable in expression.

Just the three thudding syllables I did hear.
Which will never be two or four.

Acknowledgments
(SOME POEMS REVISED & SOME RE-TITLED)

My deep appreciation to Ken, for his love and passion, and his support for the all and everything. I would like to thank Janet Holmes for her editorial intelligence, intuition, and creativity in bringing this book, and so many wonderful books, to readers. I am indebted to the wonderful poets and dear friends who gave me their wise counsel as I worked through the energies of these materials: Julie Carr, Robin Caton, Gillian Conoley, Patricia Dienstfrey, Grace Grafton, Alice Jones, Melissa Kwasny, Elizabeth Robinson, and Cassandra Smith.

American Poetry Review: two poems from "Necessities" & "Inventions" sequence; *Antennae*: "Impulse says," "History of expression"; *Black Square*: one poem from "Backward Rowing" (formerly "Facts of estrangement"), "Desire says" (formerly "Facts of appearance"); *Blue Satellite Broadsides:* "Begin again (2nd)"; *Boston Review:* "Begin again (1st)" (formerly "Prologue"); *Colorado Revew:* two poems from "Necessities" & "Inventions" sequence"; *Conduit:* "Impatience says"; *Fence:* one poem from "Backward Rowing" sequence (formerly "Facts of order & attention"); *First Intensity*: "History is hidden in fact"; *Five Fingers Review*: "History of seed," "History of sleep"; *Fourteen Hills*: "History of quiet"; *F. I. R.*: one poem from "Backward Rowing" sequence; *Interim*: one poem from "Backward Rowing" sequence, "Grace says"; *Laurel Review:* three from "Sensework" sequence; *Many Mountains Moving:* "Impatience says"; *Marsh Hawk Review Blogspot:* two poems from "Necessities" & "Inventions" sequence; *Pleiades*: one poem from "Backward Rowing" sequence (formerly "To examine a dead thing"); *Parthenon West*: two poems from "Backward Rowing" sequence; *syllogism*: "History in expression"; *untitled: a magazine of prose poetry*: "History of structure"; *VOLT*: one poem from "Backward Rowing" sequence (formerly "Necessary backward rowing"); *Xantippe*: "Patience says"; *ZYZZYVA*: one poem from "Backward Rowing" sequence (formerly "Places to look").

A selection of these poems won the Robert H. Winner Memorial Award from the Poetry Society of America.

About the Author

RUSTY MORRISON is author of *the true keeps calm biding its story,* which won the 2007 Ahsahta Press Sawtooth Poetry Prize, the Academy of American Poet's James Laughlin Award, the Northern California Book Award, and the DiCastagnola Award from Poetry Society of America, as well as three other books. *After Urgency* won The Dorset Prize from Tupelo Press; *Book of the Given* is available from Noemi Press; and *Whethering* won the Colorado Prize for Poetry. She has received the Bogin, Hemley, Winner, and DiCastagnola Awards from PSA. Her poems and/or essays have appeared or will appear in *A Pubic Space, American Poetry Review, Aufgabe, Boston Review, Gulf Coast, Kenyon Review, Lana Turner, Pleiades, Spoon River, The Volta's Evening Will Come, VOLT* and elsewhere. Her poems have been anthologized in the Norton *Postmodern American Poetry* 2nd Edition, *The Arcadia Project: Postmodern Pastoral, Beauty is a Verb,* and *The Sonnets: Translating and Rewriting Shakespeare* and elsewhere. She has been co-publisher of Omnidawn since 2001.

AHSAHTA PRESS

SAWTOOTH POETRY PRIZE SERIES

2002: Aaron McCollough, *Welkin* (Brenda Hillman, judge)

2003: Graham Foust, *Leave the Room to Itself* (Joe Wenderoth, judge)

2004: Noah Eli Gordon, *The Area of Sound Called the Subtone* (Claudia Rankine, judge)

2005: Karla Kelsey, *Knowledge, Forms, The Aviary* (Carolyn Forché, judge)

2006: Paige Ackerson-Kiely, *In No One's Land* (D. A. Powell, judge)

2007: Rusty Morrison, *the true keeps calm biding its story* (Peter Gizzi, judge)

2008: Barbara Maloutas, *the whole Marie* (C. D. Wright, judge)

2009: Julie Carr, *100 Notes on Violence* (Rae Armantrout, judge)

2010: James Meetze, *Dayglo* (Terrance Hayes, judge)

2011: Karen Rigby, *Chinoiserie* (Paul Hoover, judge)

2012: T. Zachary Cotler, *Sonnets to the Humans* (Heather McHugh, judge)

2013: David Bartone, *Practice on Mountains* (Dan Beachy-Quick, judge)

AHSAHTA PRESS

NEW SERIES

This book is set in Apollo MT type
with Perpetua Standard titles
by Ahsahta Press at Boise State University.
Cover design by Quemadura.
Book design by Janet Holmes.
Printed in Canada.

AHSAHTA PRESS

2014

JANET HOLMES, DIRECTOR

ADRIAN KIEN, ASSISTANT DIRECTOR

JERRI BENSON, *intern*   STEPHA PETERS

CHRISTOPHER CARUSO   INDRANI SENGUPTA

ZEKE HUDSON   ELIZABETH SMITH

ANNIE KNOWLES   MICHAEL WANZENRIED

ZACH VESPER